FIVE
5 FINGER
PIANO

Children's TV Favorites
Themes from 8 Hit Shows

ISBN 0-634-09380-0

HAL•LEONARD®
CORPORATION

7777 W. BLUEMOUND RD. P.O. BOX 13819 MILWAUKEE, WI 53213

Visit Hal Leonard Online at
www.halleonard.com

Barney Theme Song

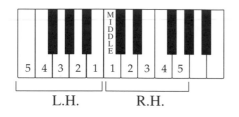

Traditional Music ("Yankee Doodle")
Lyrics by Stephen Bates Baltes
and Philip A. Parker

With spirit

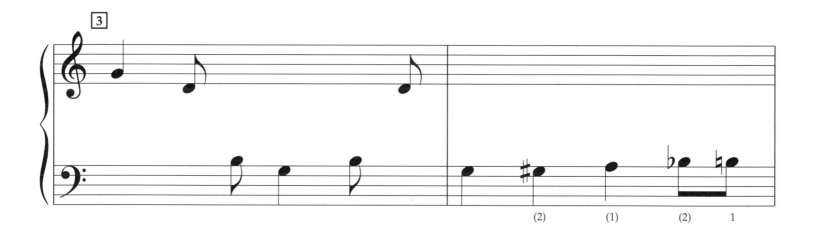

Duet Part (Student plays one octave higher than written.)

With spirit

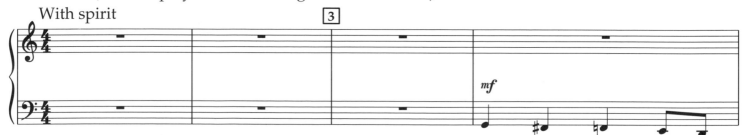

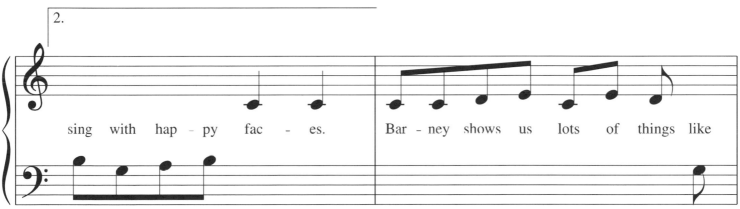

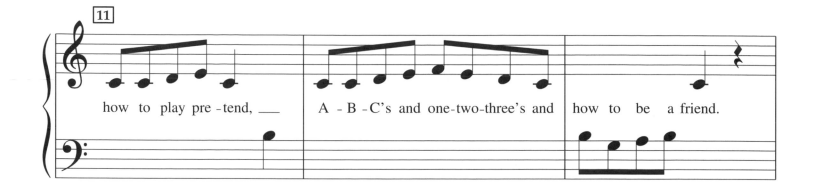

how to play pre-tend, ___ A - B - C's and one-two-three's and how to be a friend.

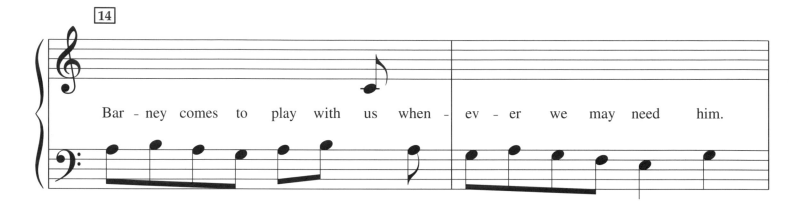

Bar - ney comes to play with us when - ev - er we may need him.

Bar - ney can be your friend too if you just make be - lieve him.

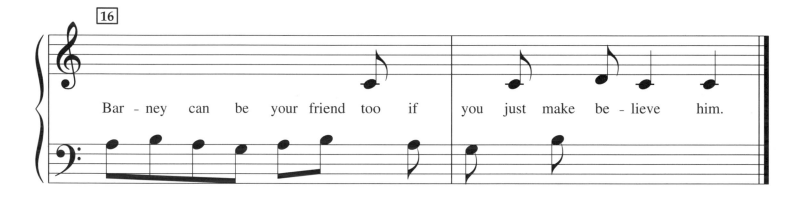

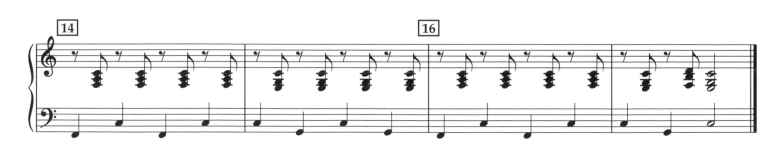

Dragon Tales Theme

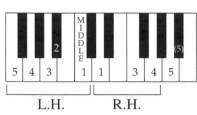

L.H.   R.H.

Words and Music by Jessee Harris,
Joey Levine and Mary Wood

Moderately fast

Em - my wished on a   drag - on scale,   that's what start - ed

mf

Drag - on Tales.   A - round the room the   drag - ons flew, but

Duet Part (Student plays one octave higher than written.)

Moderately fast

mp

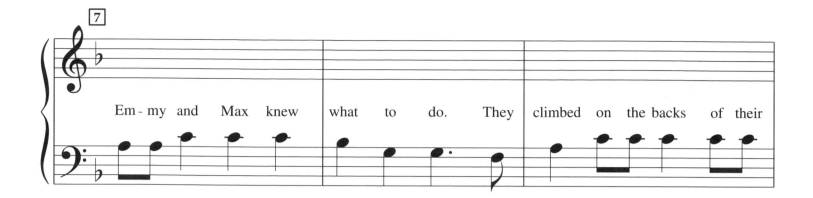

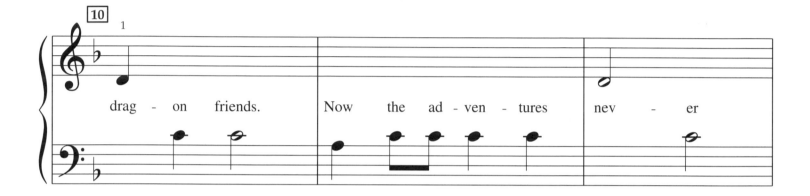

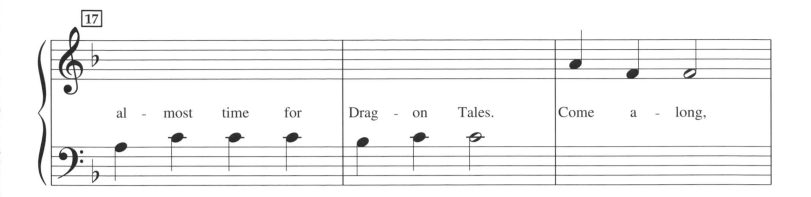

al - most time for Drag - on Tales. Come a - long,

take my hand; let's all go to Drag - on Land._____

_____ There's Ord, he's the big - gest (not so brave of heart); there's

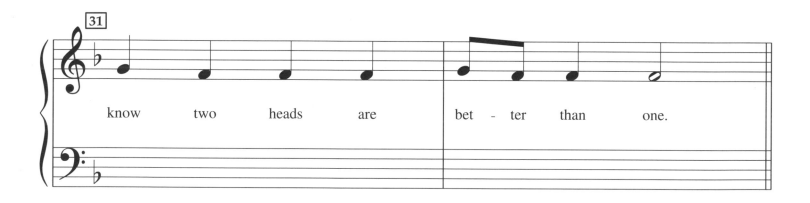

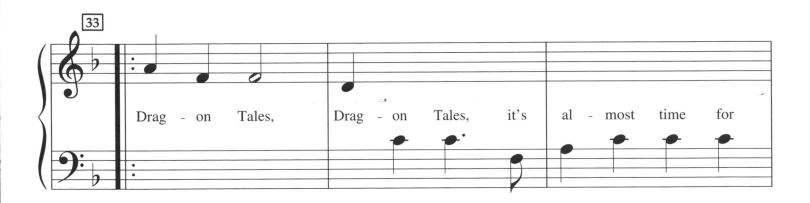

Drag - on Tales, Drag - on Tales, it's al - most time for

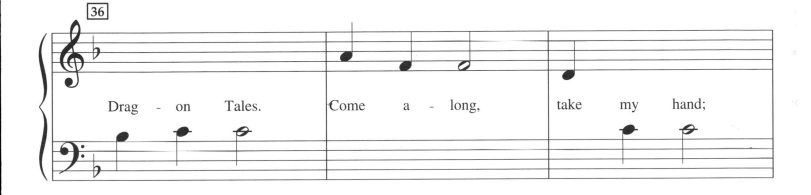

Drag - on Tales. Come a - long, take my hand;

let's all go to Drag - on Land. _____

Bob the Builder
"Intro Theme Song"

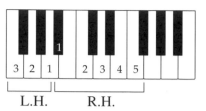

Words and Music by
Paul Joyce

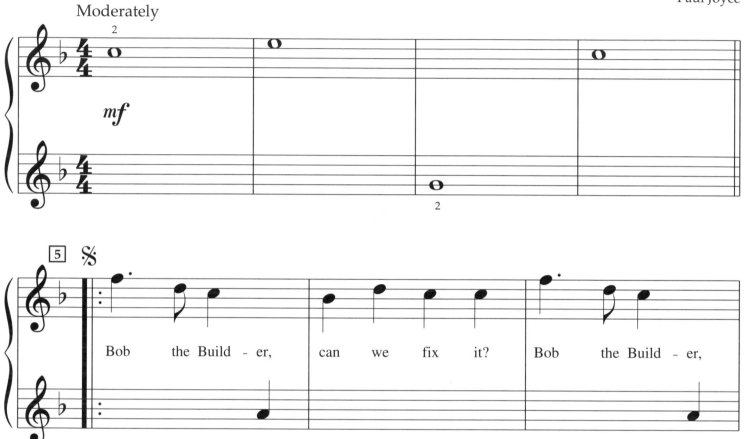

Bob   the Build - er,   can   we   fix   it?   Bob   the Build - er,

Duet Part (Student plays one octave higher than written.)

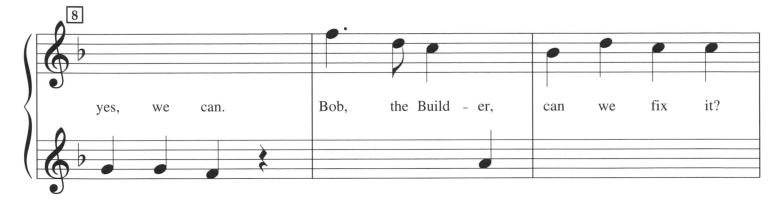

yes, we can. Bob, the Build - er, can we fix it?

Bob, the Build - er, yes, we can.
Scoop, Muck, and Diz - zy and
Time to get bus - y, such a
Dig - ging and fix - ing, hav - ing

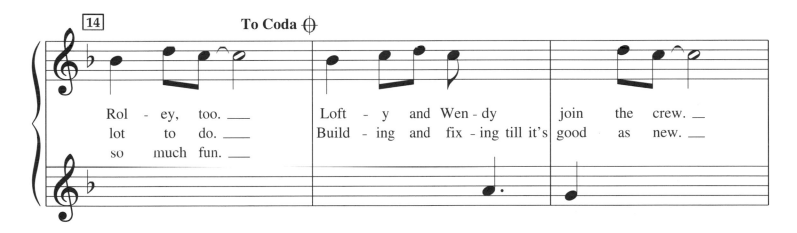

To Coda ⊕

Rol - ey, too. ___
lot to do. ___
so much fun. ___

Loft - y and Wen - dy join the crew. ___
Build - ing and fix - ing till it's good as new. ___

To Coda ⊕

Bob and the gang have so much fun, ___ work - ing to -geth -er, they
Bob and the gang make a real - ly good sound, work - ing all day till the

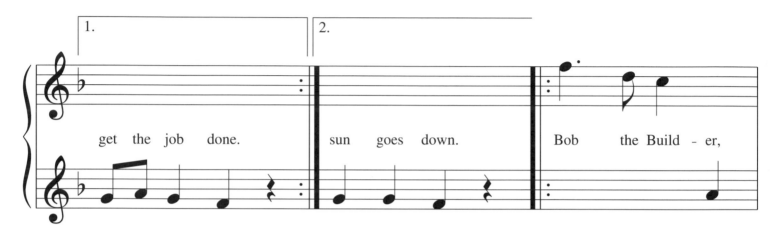

1.
get the job done.

2.
sun goes down.

Bob the Build - er,

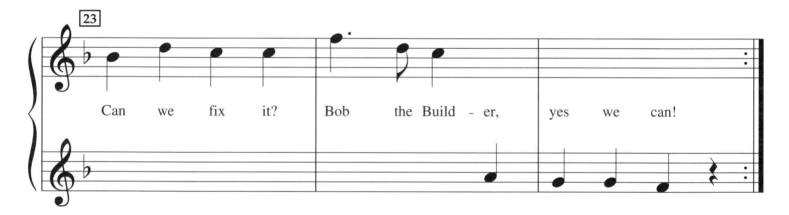

Can we fix it? Bob the Build - er, yes we can!

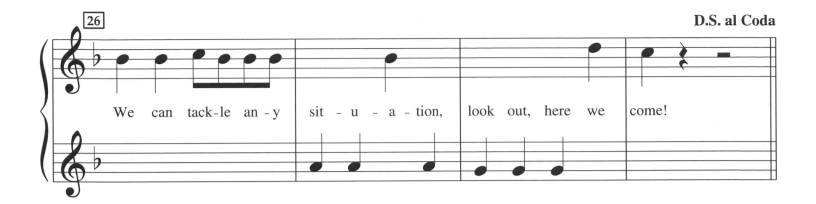

We can tack-le an-y sit - u - a - tion, look out, here we come!

CODA

Work - ing to-geth-er, they get the job done. Bob the Build - er,

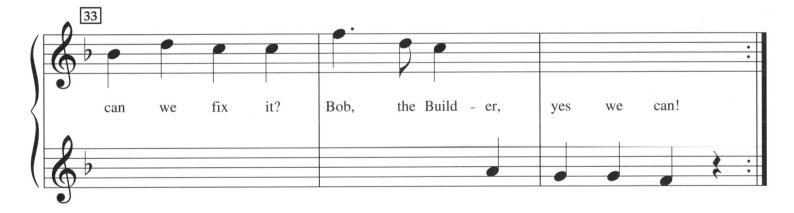

can we fix it? Bob, the Build - er, yes we can!

Dora the Explorer Theme Song

from DORA THE EXPLORER

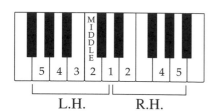

Words and Music by Josh Sitron,
Billy Straus and Sarah Durkee

Duet Part (Student plays one octave higher than written.)

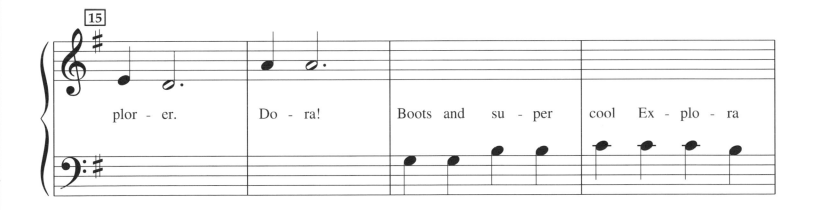

16

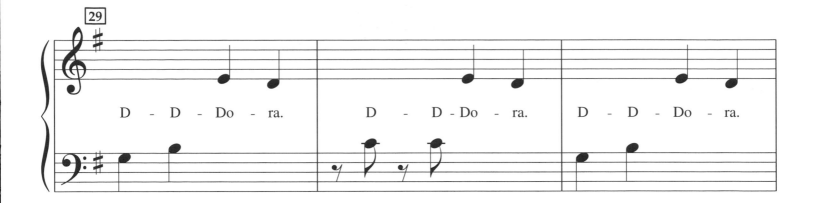

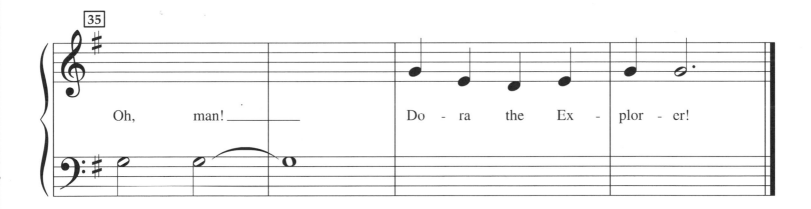

Oodelay-O
(PB&J Otter Theme Song)

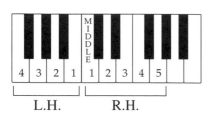

Words and Music by Dan Sawyer
and Fred Newman

Quickly, in two

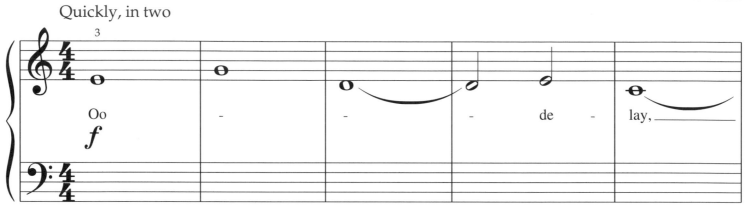

Oo - - - de - lay, _____

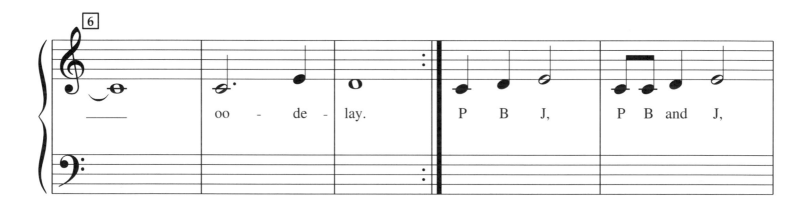

_____ oo - de - lay. P B J, P B and J,

Duet Part (Student plays one octave higher than written.)

Quickly, in two

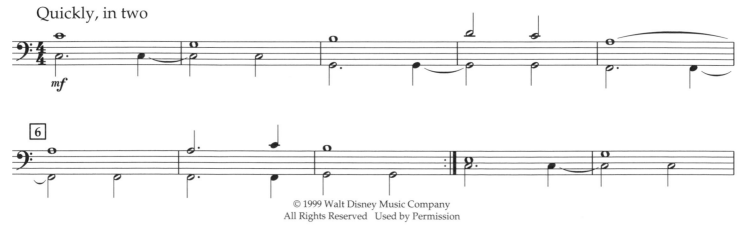

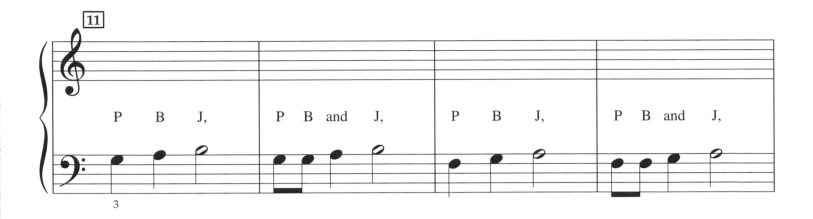

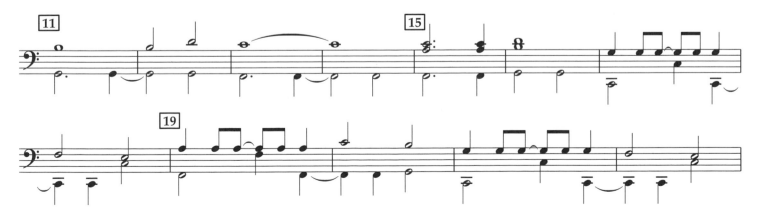

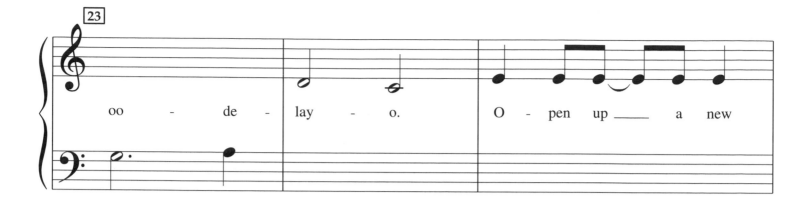

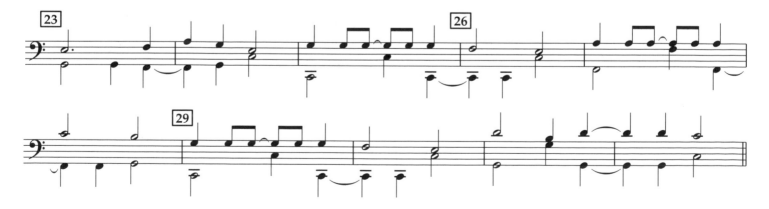

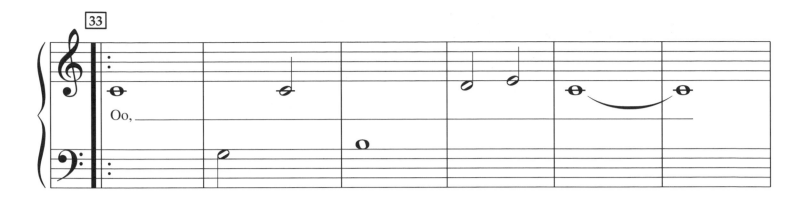

Oo,

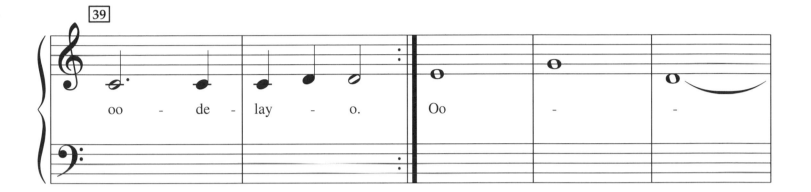

oo - de - lay - o.   Oo -

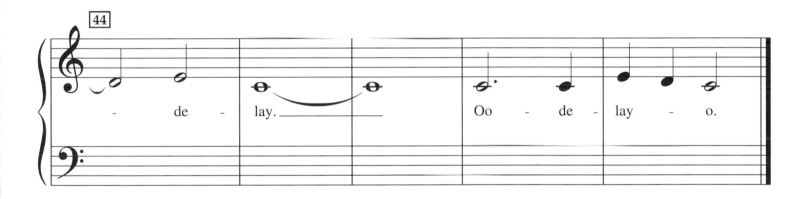

- de - lay. _____   Oo - de - lay - o.

SpongeBob SquarePants Theme Song

from SPONGEBOB SQUAREPANTS

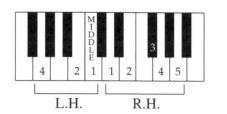

Words and Music by Mark Harrison, Blaise Smith, Steve Hillenburg and Derek Drymon

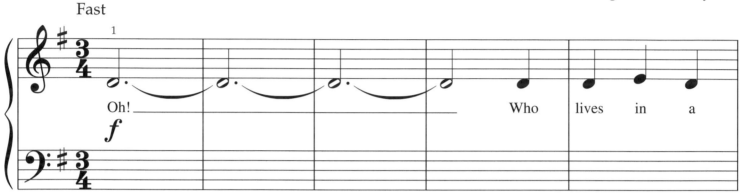

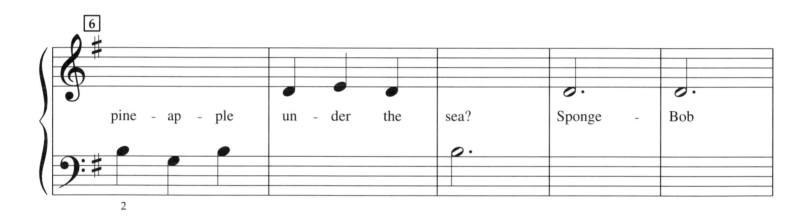

Duet Part (Student plays one octave higher than written.)

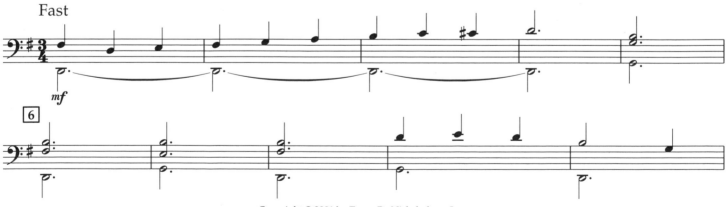

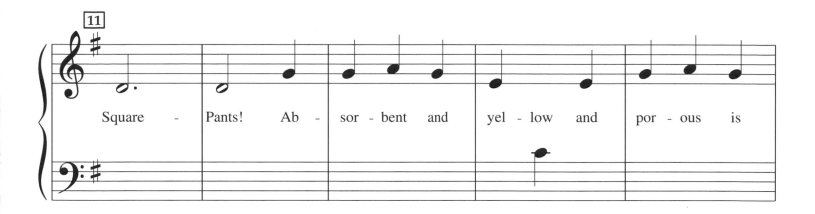

Square - Pants! Ab - sor - bent and yel - low and por - ous is

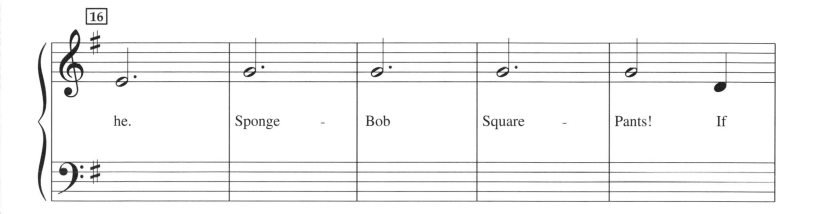

he. Sponge - Bob Square - Pants! If

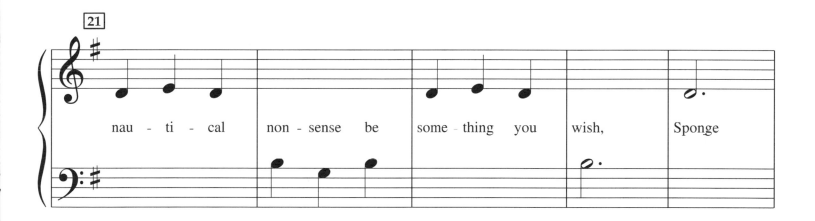

nau - ti - cal non - sense be some - thing you wish, Sponge

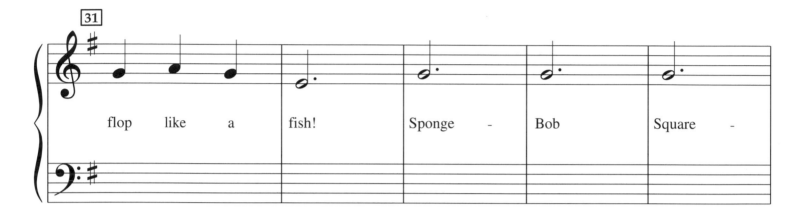

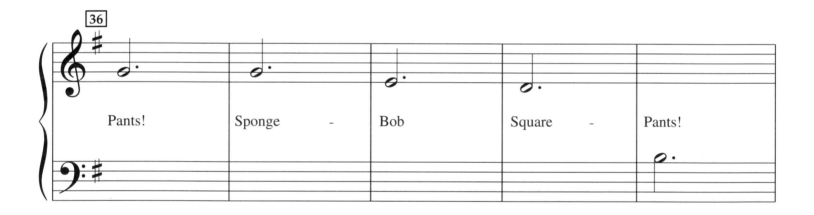

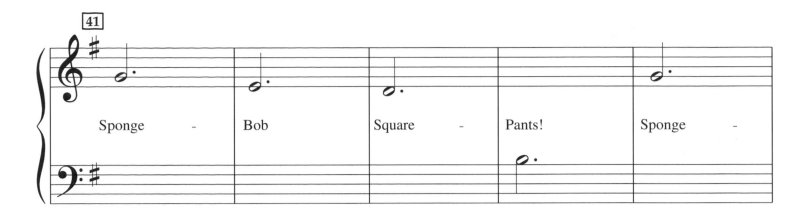

Sponge - Bob Square - Pants! Sponge -

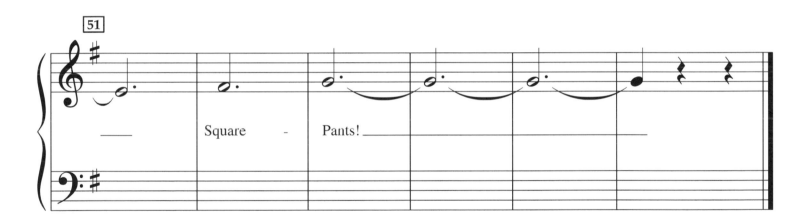

Bob Square Pants! Sponge - Bob_____

_____ Square - Pants!_____

Thomas the Tank Engine
(Main Title)
from THOMAS THE TANK ENGINE

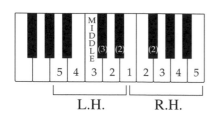

Words and Music by
Ed Welch

With a bounce

They're two, they're four, they're six, they're eight, __ shunt - ing trucks and

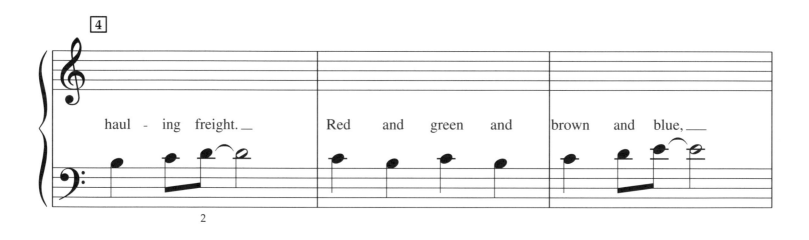

haul - ing freight. __ Red and green and brown and blue, __

Duet Part (Student plays one octave higher than written.)

With a bounce

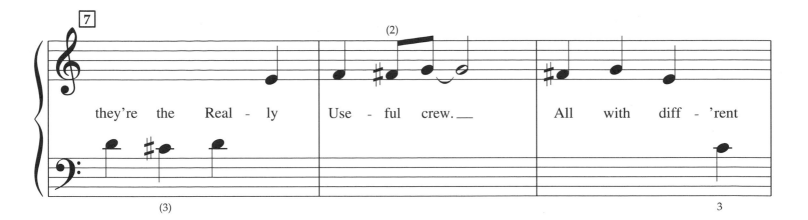

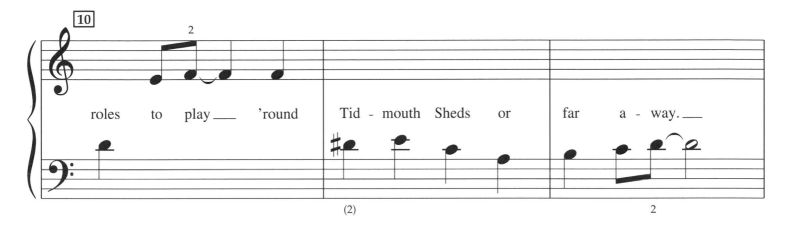

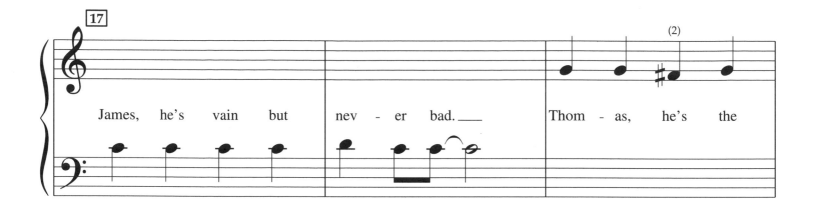

James, he's vain but nev - er bad. ___ Thom - as, he's the

(2)

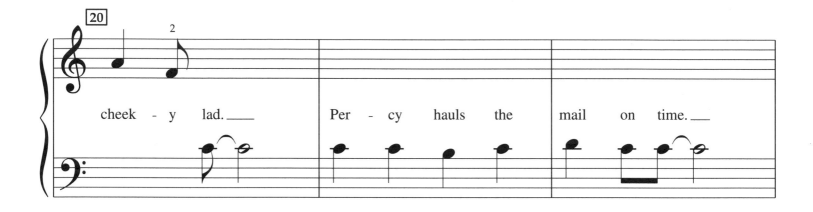

cheek - y lad. ___ Per - cy hauls the mail on time. ___

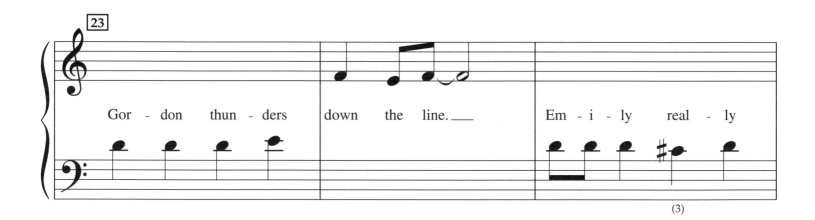

Gor - don thun - ders down the line. ___ Em - i - ly real - ly

(3)

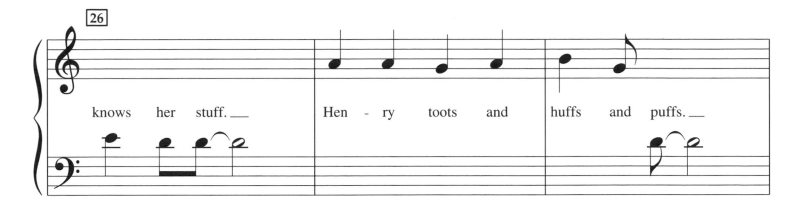

knows her stuff. ___ Hen - ry toots and huffs and puffs. ___

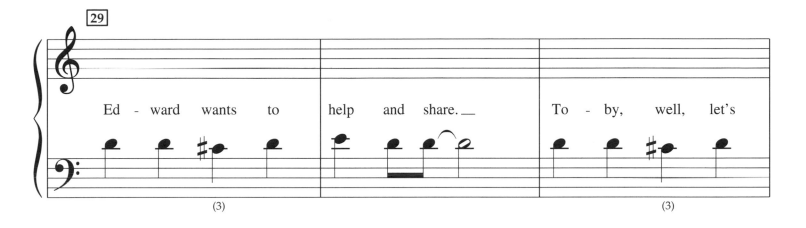

Ed - ward wants to help and share. ___ To - by, well, let's

(3)   (3)

D.S. al Fine

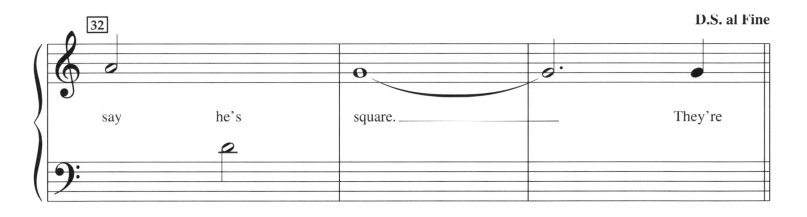

say he's square. _____ They're

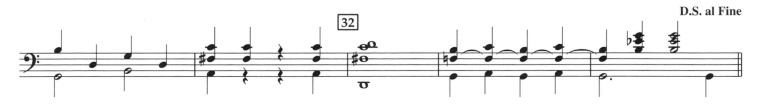

D.S. al Fine

Rugrats Theme

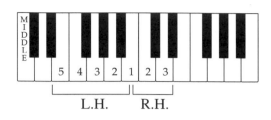

Words and Music by
Mark Mothersbaugh

Brightly

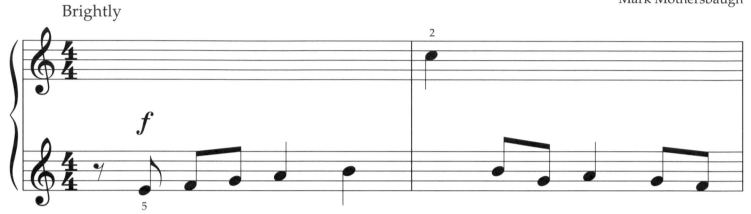

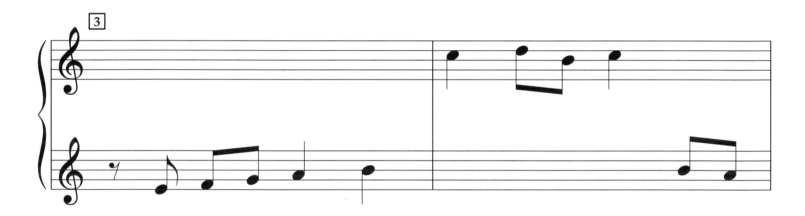

Duet Part (Student plays one octave higher than written.)

Brightly

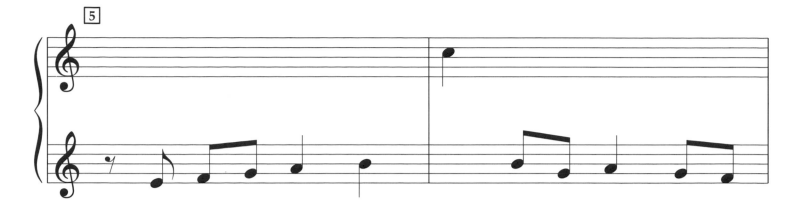

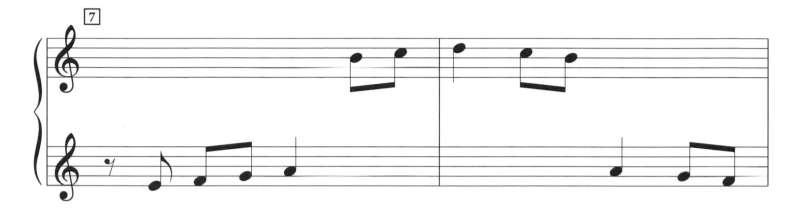

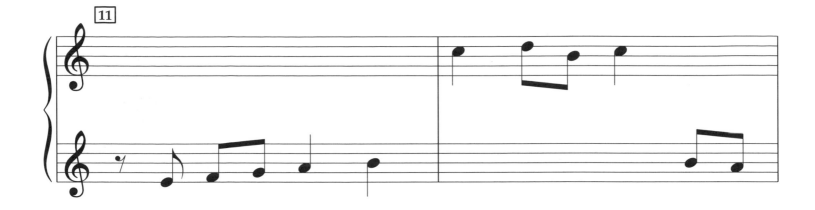

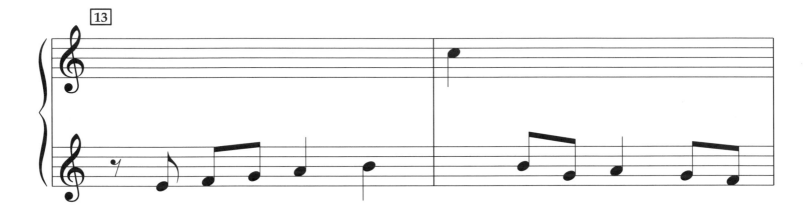

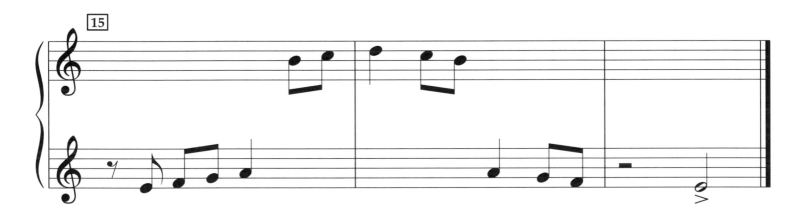